كولديلوكس والدببة الثلاثة

Goldilocks and the Three Bears

retold by Kate Clynes
illustrated by Louise Daykin

Arabic translation by Dr. Sajida Fawzi

كانت كولديلوكس تستمتع بوقتها، تقطف بعض الأزهار لأمها.
وكانت تسير بعيداً في أعماق الغابة.

توقفي كولديلوكس، عودي إلى البيت،
الغابات ليست مكاناً آمناً عندما تكونين لوحدك.

Goldilocks was having fun, collecting flowers for her mum.
She was heading **deeper** and **deeper** into the woods.

Stop Goldilocks, go back home,
Woods aren't safe when you're all alone.

وجدت كوخاً له حديقة جميلة.

"أريد أن أقطف هذه الأزهار،" قالت كولديلوكس.

"لأرى إن كان هناك أحد في البيت."

She found a cottage with a beautiful garden.
"I want to pick those flowers," said Goldilocks. "I'll see if anyone's home."

تريّثي كولديلوكس، اطرقي الباب مرة أخرى،
قد يكون ما هو شرس أو عنيف خلف الباب.

Stop Goldilocks, knock once more,
There may be something grizzly behind the door.

"هالو!" نادت كولديلوكس،
"هل في البيت أحد؟"
ولكن لم تسمع جواباً.

"Hello!" she called,
"is anybody home?"
But there was no reply.

كان على المائدة ثلاث طاسات. واحدة كبيرة الحجم،
واحدة متوسطة الحجم، وواحدة صغيرة الحجم.
"م م م م عصيدة،" قالت كولديلوكس، "أنا أكاد أموت جوعاً."

On the table were three steaming bowls. One big
bowl, one medium sized bowl and one small bowl.
"Mmmm, porridge," said Goldilocks, "I'm starving."

تريّثي كولديلوكس لا تستعجلي،
فقد تكون نتيجة الأمور مُؤذية.

Stop Goldilocks don't be hasty,
Things could turn out very nasty.

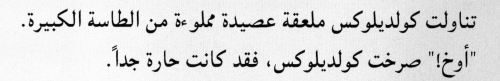

تناولت كولديلوكس ملعقة عصيدة مملوءة من الطاسة الكبيرة.

"أوخ!" صرخت كولديلوكس، فقد كانت حارة جداً.

Goldilocks took a spoonful from the big bowl.
"Ouch!" she cried. It was far too hot.

ثُمَّ ذاقت من عصيدة الطاسة المتوسطة الحجم.

"يَخْ!" فقد كانت باردة جداً.

Then she tried the middle bowl.
"Yuk!" It was far too cold.

ولكن العصيدة في الطاسة الصغيرة كانت
مناسبة جداً فأكلت كولديلوكس منها كثيراً!

The small bowl, however, was just
right and Goldilocks ate the lot!

وبعد شعورها بالشبع والإرتياح، تجوّلت
ودخلت الغرفة المجاورة.

With a nice full tummy, she
wandered into the next room.

تمهّلي كولديلوكس، لا يمكنك أن تتجوّلي هكذا،
وتتطفّلي على شؤون بيت الآخرين.

Hang on Goldilocks, you can't just roam,
And snoop around someone else's home.

كان في الغرفة ثلاثة كراسٍ
أمام النار الموقدة الدافئة.
واحد كبير الحجم، واحد متوسط الحجم
ووواحد صغير الحجم.

In front of the warm, glowing fire
were three chairs.
One big chair, one medium sized
chair and one small chair.

جلست كولديلوكس أولاً على الكرسي الكبير، ولكنه كان صلباً جداً.

ثُمّ جلست على الكرسي المتوسط الحجم، ولكنه كان ليّناً جداً.

ولكن الكرسي الصغير كان مناسباً جداً.

وحين استرخت عليه كولديلوكس ...

First Goldilocks climbed onto the big chair, but it was
just too hard.
Then she climbed onto the medium sized chair,
but it was just too soft.
The little chair, however, felt just right.
Goldilocks was leaning back, when...

فجأة! تكسّرت سيقان الكرسي
وسقطت كولديلوكس على الأرض.
"أووخ،" صاحت كولديلوكس.
"ياله من كرسي سخيف!"

أووه، لا كولديلوكس، ماذا فعلتِ؟
انهضي سريعاً، انهضي واهربي.

SNAP! The legs broke
and she fell onto the floor.
"Ouch," she cried.
"Stupid chair!"

Oh no Goldilocks, what have you done?
Get up quick, get up and run.

وشعرت كولديلوكس بالتعب فأخذت طريقها إلى الطابق العلوي. وفي غرفة النوم وجدت ثلاثة أسِرّة. سرير كبير الحجم، سرير متوسط الحجم وسرير صغير الحجم.

Goldilocks felt tired so she made her way upstairs.
In the bedroom were three beds.
One big bed, one medium sized bed and one small bed.

جرّبت السرير الكبير ولكنه كان مُكعبراً.
ثُمّ جرّبت السرير المتوسط الحجم وكان كثير الزنبركات.
ولكنها وجدت السرير الصغير مناسباً جداً
وسرعان ما نامت نوماً عميقاً.

She climbed up onto the big bed but it was too lumpy.
Then she tried the medium sized bed, which was too
springy. The small bed however, felt just right
and soon she was fast asleep.

استيقظي كولديلوكس، افتحي عينيك.
فقد يكون في انتظارك مفاجأة كبيرة!

Wake up Goldilocks, open your eyes,
You could be in for a BIG surprise!

وفي الوقت نفسه عادت الدببة الثلاثة
إلى البيت. وعند دخوله عثر الدب الأب
بسلة، ولفتت المائدة انتباهه.

Just then the three bears came home.
After tripping over a basket,
Father Bear noticed the table.

"لقد أكل أحد عصيدتي،" قال الدب الأب
بصوت عالٍ مبحوح.
"لقد أكل أحد عصيدتي،" ردّدت
الدبة الأم بصوت معتدل.

"Someone's been eating my porridge," he said
in a loud gruff voice.
"Someone's been eating my porridge," echoed
Mother Bear in a medium voice.

"لقد أكل أحد عصيدتي،" صاح الدب الصغير قائلاً بصوت ناعم،
"لقد أُكِلت كلّها!"

"Someone's been eating my porridge," cried Baby Bear in a small voice,
"and they've eaten it all up!"

كانت الدببة الثلاثة في غاية الجوع وشيء من الإرهاق،
ولكن سلة أزهار ذلك المخلوق الغريب
لم تبدُ مخيفة جداً بالنسبة لها.

Three very hungry bears, feeling slightly wary,
But a flower-collecting monster
doesn't sound too scary.

وأمسكت الدببة الثلاثة أيدي بعضها البعض

وتوجّهت ببطء وهدوء نحو غرفة الجلوس.

"لقد جلس أحد على كرسيّي،" قال الدبّ الأب بصوت عالٍ مبحوح.

"لقد جلس أحد على كرسيّي،" قالت الدبة الأم بصوت معتدل.

Holding hands, they crept into the living room.
"Someone's been sitting in my chair,"
said Father Bear in a loud gruff voice.
"Someone's been sitting in my chair,"
echoed Mother Bear in a medium voice.